Dear adults
we have issues too!

Stories of life lessons taught at an early age to preteens and teenagers who refuse to give up!

This book is
dedicated to
every child
who holds their
story within.

Contributing**Authors**

Semaj Washington

Syhion Washington

Kilani Harvey

Unyque King

Zacheriah Andre

Jalia Simmons

Shakia Simmons

Brashaya McCrimmon-Lampkin

Zaniyah Starke

Amilina Villafane

Contents

Dear adults,

What you're holding in your hands right now is not a collection of words strung into beautiful sentences.
Its hearts laid open...

It's a journey through life and finding healing. It's an invitation extended to share a table with a young one's inner soul its stories of life lessons taught at an early age to preteens and teenagers who refuse to give up! Trust me when I say this – It wasn't easy compiling this book. It wasn't easy for the young authors to revisit their reality and share their journey through words, as most of them had repressed their emotions and hide them under their everyday thoughts; years and years of thoughts. But healing took place. Because of this book many, for the first time, openly shared their stories and rode the journey to find their healing. In fact, during the process, one of our young authors lost her mother to unexpected death. But she continued to go on. Life isn't easy, neither for adults nor children.

Some life lessons are learned from others, but some are our own, and we must experience something's to get to the lesson. A few of our young authors had the support of their family and others to help them endure their journeys. However, some had to jump through hoops alone.

Adults, I know that you are providing for all your child's needs. However, it does not take away the fact that your child fights a battle within, every day! At times, they muster the courage to speak to you about it, but often, keep it to themselves. As the compiler of this book, I promised every child that I would share this truth with all adults, be they parents, aunts, uncles, older friends, or mentors. Children, tweens, and teens have issues too." So, I request you to be more open-minded. I request you to be willing to hear their voices and be more receptive to their mental and emotional struggles.

Let's expel the fact that children and young adults should not or do not have issues, because they do, regardless of their age, demographics, status quo, or environment. I'm sure, in your formative years, you too had a few of your own.

I sincerely hope this book serves as a gentle reminder that everyone is dealing with their issues and all we need is a bit more compassion.

Children, tweens, and teens have issues too.

"Fighting"
It's not the way
to success and
will not bring
back my dad!

- Semaj Washington

Lesson Learned

" I learned that fighting in school is not the best way to show that I was hurting."

However the reporting of this tragedy was so. I remember when I got trouble in school so much in 3rd and 4th grade and my mom would have to come to the school. She would have to come to the office because of me fighting almost every week.

One day, I got into a fight with a boy over some markers and I threw him across the table and then I got suspended because I got into fights too many times. Because of the suspension, I missed field day and my mom had to work so, I had to go to the Air Force Base and do work the entire day. When I came back to school the following week, I was told I had to sit in a corner because I was not allowed to talk to anyone so that I would not want to get into any fights.

I had to get my hair cut a lot for punishment and I don't like cutting my hair. For fighting in school so much my punishment was to sleep outside on the back patio and live like a homeless person to learn the hard way about why I needed to stop getting in trouble.

When I had to sleep outside, I felt sad and I felt like that was what I was supposed to be because that's where my mom told me that, I was going to end up if I kept on acting up in school and I didn't want to end up living outside and having spiders crawling on me and

I cried all night. I wanted to be in the house with my family and sleeping in my bed with a pillow and not a sleeping bag and I would like to have more than just a peanut butter jelly sandwich and water. When my mom told me to go sleep outside I didn't want to but I had to. In my head, I said I hated her and wanted to kill her because I was so mad at her and I didn't like her at that time.

From my punishments, I learned not to fight in school because I did not want to be a homeless person. I overcame fighting in school by not trying to be a class clown and also thinking about how I felt from my punishments and how my mom felt about me fighting in school. I felt like my mom was giving up on me. I thought my mom wasn't going to take care of me anymore or like me anymore because I was a bad kid but I overcame that and I started to get my act right and I passed FSA.

My mom put me in a different school to start a better school year and gave me a fresh start with new kids. I felt like a different person in the 5th grade because when I was in third grade, I felt like I wasn't trying to learn, I felt like I was choosing to not learn and it feels good to actually be learning in school and truly feeling like I have my mom on my side believing in me and helping me with my homework and stuff.

When I was getting into all that trouble in school, I felt like I was just a bad kid and I didn't belong in school and I felt like school wasn't the right place for me.

From me getting in trouble in school, my teachers started to make me feel like whatever I did I was going to get in trouble. Even for small things like sharpening three pencils when the maximum was two or for telling one of them to slow down and teach. My teachers started sending me to the office for everything.

In 4th grade, I couldn't learn with my teacher teaching so fast and not explaining, so I told her she was teaching too fast and that she was trying to rush through the lessons. I told my mom and she decided to come sit in my classroom to see how fast she was teaching. Even my mom said that she was actually teaching super-fast. My mom asked her why was she teaching so fast, she said she was trying to rush the lessons because we were five months behind and the FSA was coming up. But I wasn't able to learn and I wasn't able to understand what she was teaching. When I told my teacher she was teaching too fast I think that she was thinking that I was trying to be a class clown because I got in trouble so much for trying to make people laugh before but I wasn't and it still ended up with me getting in trouble.

One reason I think I was fighting at school so much was because I was just trying to be a class clown and if people didn't think my jokes on them were funny they would push me and try to fight with me. I remember my dad always used to tell me "You have no friends in school because you're not going to remember them when you grow up later on in your life".

I think my dad used to tell me that because he said I was the spitting image of him when it comes to school and wanting to be the center

of attention and that I had his attitude. I think he told me that to keep me from going down the same road that he went when he was younger, like going to jail and having to live on the streets. I think my mom was so hard on me in school because she doesn't want me to end up having a bad reputation for fighting in school and not having a life. She told me if I go to jail she's not going to visit me because she told me not to be a class clown and stop fighting in school.

The other reason. I meant the big reason I was fighting so much in school is something I never told my mom. The reason is, I was fighting in school because I was mad at my dad for passing away and I missed him so, I thought fighting in school would bring him back but it didn't. It just made things worse for me. It wasn't until fourth grade I realized fighting was not going to bring my dad back. My fourth-grade teacher asked me "Why are you fighting?" I said I was mad at my dad and she said: "it's not going to bring him back, you need to be good in school to make him proud and it hurts your mom to see you getting in so much trouble." "Thank You" to my 4th-grade teacher for telling me this.

Now that I am older, I think my best way of honoring my parents is bringing home good grades to show that I've been listening to them and taking in all the things that they've been telling me to do.

Basically what I'm trying to say is getting in trouble and fighting in school is not a good thing because you're going to end up having a lot of people not liking you and you thinking people are your friends and then it turns out their not your friends, you can end up in the corner sitting by yourself and then everyone's talking about you even the teachers might send you to the office for doing something that wasn't that serious like sharpening too many pencils so stay out of trouble and don't fight. I learned that fighting in school is not the best way to show that I was hurting. I think I should've just told my mom and my brother the reason why I was fighting in school and that I was hurting.

From me getting my act together in school, I was able to start S2T2 Sports Apparel, LLC with my brother and I've been able to play sports. I have been able to stay in the house and also have a bed to sleep in and have a roof over my head and my mom actually on my side.

I have my own business-S2T2 to honor my dad and help my mom. I am the Senior Executive Officer and I mostly do the sewing of our apparel. This is cool to do because I get to see kids all over Orlando mostly wearing my brand. What I like most about my business is; I am making my own money, it keeps me busy, and I get to make new apparel. Because of my business, I am not just sitting around the house waiting to get in trouble. I try not to get in trouble in school because I do not want to put a bad reputation on my business. There is so much to know about how much I have changed and how my brand got started.

My message to you

With my story and brand, I want to inspire other kids to pursue their dreams and make their parents happy. If you are one of those kids that were like me when I was in 3rd and 4th grade, I would advise you stop doing the bad things that you're doing because you're going to end up either dying because people don't like you or you having to live on a street and you wouldn't want that. You want to have a happy family with a wife. I want kids to know that fighting is not the way to success and will not bring back the dead.

Semaj Washington

11 Years Old

You can read more at
www.s2t2sportsapparel.com
or go check out our

s2t2sportsapparel

"Deal with your grief to get through your struggles"

- Syhion Washington

Lesson Learned

"I'm thankful for sports and thankful for my music and thankful for all people that helped me. I'm thankful for these people because I know if I didn't have their support I probably would've been depressed... No, very depressed and probably wouldn't have been able to bounce back from it but thanks to sports, my family, and music I've been able to deal more with my grief."

I was eight years old when I was told my dad passed away. When I first found out, I didn't really believe that he was gone. I wouldn't let myself believe that he was gone! My mom told me that when she first told me, I didn't even cry or look sad.

It didn't actually set in that my dad passed away until I saw his casket being lowered into the ground. In my mind, I was thinking he was going to come back or just show up out of nowhere miraculously. I remember when I first found out, I was mad at my mom because I thought she was lying to me. In my head, I was thinking "why would she lie about something like that". But after my father's funeral, I started to get dreams of him telling me that he was alive and that he was ok. But every time I woke up from those dreams I cried because I realized that he wasn't really here.

I am 14 and now when I look back at it, I realize that was his way of telling me that he was Ok. I believe that now he gives me and my younger brother little hints that he is still in our lives, sometimes when me and my brother have sports events that make us nervous or go through hard times his favorite song always comes on the radio. Sometimes, I get angry at him because he isn't here but I know he couldn't control it.

After my dad has passed, I had some problems with myself and struggled at home with being angry a lot and catching attitudes but surprisingly it never affected my school life. It did, however, affect me by stopping me from being a big brother. I wasn't being much of a role model at all, I was actually very mad with everything and everybody. I was doing everything I wasn't supposed to do, like not following rules catching an attitude and being disrespectful and I think it was because I was mad and angry... No, I was sad but I was holding it in which made it come out as anger. I feel like I was getting in a lot of trouble with my mother because I was being very disrespectful and not following rules. I didn't want to do anything and my mom is very family oriented. She always wants all of us to do something together but at that time, I didn't want to do anything. I just wanted to sit in my room and watch TV. But she wouldn't allow that which made me mad.

I feel like if I would've just been out front with my feelings and let them out, none of this would've happened. I would've still been sad but I would have let it out and it would have come out as more of like me trying to get help but I was just mad for no reason. Actually, there was a reason I was holding my sadness and it was making me mad.

Knowing how my dad was; he probably would've told me I need to let them know what's going on because if you don't let them know you can't get help and he probably would've said you need to go find something to occupy yourself with, something that makes you happy or you will always be mad all the time.

I try to keep in mind my dad gave me the nickname Champ because he knew that I needed to live by that name and knows that I am the CHAMP. My mom told me the story about how my dad wanted to name me Lion at first because he wanted me to be known as a king, fearless, and tough. My mom wanted to name me Zion. She got him to agree on Syhion which was a combination of the two names. One night, I had a nightmare, and I asked my dad what are you doing here? All he said was "your name is Champion and your last name is Washington and a Washington face whatever obstacles that come their way so, know you'll get through them." This started to give me the strength to deal with my obstacles.

To overcome what I was going through I got my mind back into sports like track and I started to play musical instruments more. I recently started to open up to my family about what was going on inside of me. I feel like I'm not done grieving but I'm not grieving as hard as I was before and I'm not holding it in anymore. I'm getting stronger and being a better role model to my brother. I am now trying my best not to get an attitude with both my mom and brother. I've started telling my mom what's going on with me more.

If I didn't start dealing with my grief, I probably would've been a more troubled kid, and I would have been even angrier. Now that I've started to deal with my grief, I am becoming happier, and I'm not doing the same things I was before, and now I can help my brother when he's going through stuff.

I feel that now that I have my business with my brother, it is showing how strong I have become and how all of my pain and struggle is becoming something good. I want my pain, struggles and young businessmen success to help others in the future as well as continuing to help myself. I don't think of my business as a negative reminder of my grief, I see my business as an outcome of my grief.

If my dad was here on earth, he'd be really happy about what I'm doing. He would have even had a part of what I'm doing. He would probably be at every single Sporting and Business event. My dad would've been taking so many pictures and doing everything for us.

To others that may be grieving, let it out and tell someone how you feel. This will stop you from balling it up. Balling it up, you can only take so much, and when you reach your limit it's going to come out in a very bad way. I would recommend finding something to occupy your time that would take your mind off of it. One way is to think positive thoughts and only positive thoughts because the more negative you think, the angrier you get on the inside.

Sports helped me to deal with my grief because it's a way for me to let my anger out. I started using Track to let some of my anger out in my races. But sometimes when I'm running I do wish my dad was here but I know that he's always here in sprit.

My brother and I have a business brand called S2T2 Sports Apparel, which is "Strength to the Second Power". Our business is a way for us to honor our dad and ourselves and also show how far we've gone and that we were able to open a business and get stuff done on our own. Strength To The Second Power comes from us showing strength unknown even though we are still grieving, we are getting through it and still able to maintain our own business turning something bad into something good. I am the Chief Executive Officer and I mostly do the customization of our apparel.

'm thankful for having people to help me grieve. am thankful for my mom doing everything she can to help me grieve even though she was grieving at the same time. I'm thankful for sports and thankful for my music and thankful for all people that helped me. I'm thankful for these people because I know if I didn't have their support I probably would've been depressed... No, very depressed and probably wouldn't have been able to bounce back from it but thanks to sports, my family, and music I've been able to deal more with my grief.

My favorite thing my dad ever told me is; you do everything with the heart, you fight with your heart, love with your heart, you play with your heart...do everything with your heart, and I use that every day because I play sports in my heart. I try to do everything with my heart because I know that, that's what he wanted me to do and that's what he left me with.

My message to you

I hope everybody reading this receives what I've said and benefited from what I've gone through and with their heart use my situation to get through it. Because you have someone looking forward to you making it through your grief. You can do this, don't give up! Keep the legacy of your loved ones alive by being the best person you can be.

You can read more at
www.s2t2sportsapparel.com
or go check out our

s2t2sportsapparel

Syhion
Washington

14 Years Old

Difference Is My Name

- Kilani Harvey

Lesson Learned

"I want everyone that is reading this to always remember that you can overcome any of life's obstacles; all it takes is faith in your ability, belief in yourself, determination, hard work and a dream."

My name is Kilani Harvey and I am 17 years old. I'm the eldest girl of five children in a single parent home; I have three brothers and one sister. The past 3 years has been quite overwhelming as my family has been nomadically drifting from location to location in search of a stable home in the poverty stricken Parramore community in Orlando, FL. Not only has this issue placed financial stress on my family and me, but it has drifted us apart and left me with no moral support as well. One of the things I pride myself on is that I will be a first-generation college student. It's been a battle transferring from a private Christian school to a public school, but I fought through it.

As for my life, I have plans and goals that I strive to achieve. My desire is to work very hard to obtain a full ride scholarship to college. I want to make a difference and I want to be a great example for my younger siblings. I take school very seriously, I have dreams and goals for the future that I am determined to make happen, and I don't expect anyone to do the work for me. I come from what is an increasingly normal background: my parents are separated and I live with my mom and siblings. What makes me different from the rest of the crowd is how I choose to spend my spare time while away from school. I come from a low-income family, so I've always

known that I'd have to get a job during the summer and after school to help with my college funding.

See, growing up in my neighborhood, it's unlikely for you to just know what you will become later in life. But I knew from the very start, that I was destined for greatness. It would either be my grades that would help me succeed and make it out of the hood or these long, dark skinned legs that were made for running. That's right; I knew I'd be a track star! Most people often believed that I was fast and for a while I believed I was doing things I was supposed to do, but my mind was always made up to be the difference. Even hanging out with certain friends; I always created boundaries and separated myself when things would get out of hand because I know that I have a future to look forward to.

Instead of getting the easiest job I could find, like many of my friends, I purposely sought out work that would teach me new skills as well as give me a sense of fulfillment. Every summer I work as a Summer Camp Youth Counselor and I help the kids in my community not only by observing the way that they interact with each other but I also make sure that they are playing with skill and determination. I also help them to learn valuable life lessons such as, how to be a good teammate and friend, as well as how to settle disputes fairly and efficiently.

I've always considered myself to be a positive and successful individual. I am especially proud of this because I don't naturally excel in all subjects. Math has always been a challenge for me because I find variables, fractions, and word problems to often be confusing, but I have learned through my involvement with many varsity level sports that quitting never feels as good as conquering your own fears. During my 11th-grade year, my coach challenged me in track when a new girl joined the Jones track team. I ran the 100-meter dash, the 200-meter dash, the 4x100 relay and I did the long jump. My coach took me out of the 4x100 relay and 100-meter dash and gave my place to the new runner and he made me run the 400 meter relay. I was so hurt, because I love running the 4x100 relay, that's my favorite race. My coach knew that the only way to convince me to run the 400 meter relay was to force me into it, because I would not have run it on my own. No matter how much I cried about it, I fought through it, I ran the 400 meter relay and got my place back on the 4x100 relay and I beat my personal record in the 200-meter dash with a 26.01.

That experience taught me a lot because my coach would get upset with me and tell me that I don't understand how much potential I have and how great I can be. He would tell me that it's my mentality that stops me and not my ability. These are words that I will carry with me no matter where I go in life. I want everyone that is reading this to always remember that you can overcome any of life's obstacles; all it takes is faith in your ability, belief in yourself, determination, hard work and a dream.

When you look for me, know that Difference is my name!

Kilani
Harvey

Is this my Life?

- Unyque King

"The crowd went crazy, and I was so proud of myself. My mom was so surprised to see me do a solo; she was smiling and said "I didn't know you could do all that!" She knew then that I was serious about dancing, and said that she was going to put me in a dance group. Its memories like this, that I will always keep with me."

My life has been hard; there's no way around it. Once upon a time, not that long ago, my family and I were homeless and we had to stay with other people. It was so hard for my mom, because she was getting sick and had to keep going to the hospital to get her strength back. It was hard trying to take care of 7 kids by herself. My mom had no one by her side that really cared enough; no one by her side to keep her going every day.

My mom suffered from high blood pressure and I always felt so bad for her because it hurt to hear her say things like, "I'm trying hard to make it for y'all." Every time my mom would ask me to help her or rub her feet I would do it, because I love her and wanted her to feel better. Sometimes I would hear my mom saying that I am the one who is going to help her when she gets old and I agree because I want her to be happy. No matter what situation you may be in your mom is always there, well most times mom's are always there. Your mom loves you and wants the best for you. No matter how hard life got, my mom would always pray and believe that things would get better.

So, I wrote everything you just read in May of 2019. This is so sad for me to look at now, because I never knew how good I really had it back then. On July 7, 2019 my mother died

unexpectedly, and my whole world change. I think she died from being stressed out and working hard to take care of us. When I look back, I know how hard it was for my mom, but I didn't think that she would die.

My mom was an awesome mother and she loved us all so much. Lately, I find myself crying a lot and I get sad anytime someone mentions my mother. Can you believe that people at my school really bring up my mother just to make me mad? I get so angry and sometimes I even curse at them, and one time I almost fought a girl and a boy for picking on me about my mom. People can be so mean, but I often think about what my mom would have told me to do. My mom would have said, "Nene, don't worry about what they are saying, just keep going and try to ignore them." "But if they put their hands on you, Beat Dat a$$!" I'm just being honest.

Even writing this is making me smile, as I think about how my mom really was. So as I try to heal from this, I am taking therapy and I cry any time I feel like it. This is hard, but my mom would have expected me to be strong. One of the things that I got from my mom was her makeup. She loved makeup, and now I get to play in her makeup with my sisters. My mom knew that I was writing this story and, guess what.... she even helped me write the first part of it. She told me to finish writing my story, and that she would read it when it was done. So, now I'm wondering if she can read my story from Heaven. Knowing her, she is and that's why I had to finish it. See, I know my mom is peaceful now, and in a calm place. I know that she worked hard for us to have things, and loved us a whole lot. I am going to miss her, but I plan to make her happy no matter what.

I use to tell her that I wanted to be a lawyer, a makeup artist, a teacher, a nail tech and so many other things. She supported my dreams 100%. She loved to see me dance and step. One of my best performances was for the Martin Luther King parade in January of 2019. My mom walked with my youth center and I for the parade and I was with my step team. At one part during the walk while in the parade, I was asked to do a solo dance, but I had no routine to do. I was so nervous and I kept breathing hard, trying to calm myself down because there were so many people watching. After a few breaths, I started dancing slowly and soon got into the rhythm and I danced like I was Beyonce! The crowd went crazy, and I was so proud of myself. My mom was so surprised to see me do a solo; she was smiling and said "I didn't know you could do all that!" She knew then that I was serious about dancing, and said that she was going to put me in a dance group.

Its memories like this, that I will always keep with me. I plan to keep a respectful attitude with adults, because my mother expected that from me. She would always say "Nene fix ya attitude." I plan to do well in school and make good grades, because I know that she would have wanted this for me. People always tell me that I look just like my momma, and I am glad about that. I'm not going to say that I will do everything perfect, but I will do my best. I know for sure that my mom is watching over me.

If you are reading my story and you have lost someone that is special to you, I hope that you are able to see that you are not the only one. My advice to you would be to: 1. Be strong, 2. Keep your head up (well at least that's what people tell me to do), and 3. It's ok to cry and it's ok to show your feelings, (although I haven't learned how to do this yet). Momma I dedicate this story to you, because you helped me to get it started. You were so happy for me to be the youngest author in this book, and even though you are gone from this earth, I am still trying to make you smile. I love you Momma, Rest Peacefully.
In memory of my mom Ms. China Lowe

Unyque
King

12 Years Old

I still wouldn't change a thing!

- Zachariah Andre

Lesson Learned

"I've learned that you can't rush love, love is blind, not everyone knows how to love, and most of all that love is complicated."

As I've gotten older, I have learned to look back on the good times and the simple times, as well as the completely miserable times. Everyone is happy when times are good, we usually take the simple moments for granted, and we tend to dread the miserable times. However, every single one of these events has played a role in molding us into the people that we are today. Personally, it's been the most miserable times that have influenced me the most. When I take a step back and I look at the bigger picture, I see the miserable times for what they truly are: challenges, or opportunities to learn and grow in many aspects.

The Challenge, being raised by a single mother, there are five of us. The oldest was my sister Taliah who actually ended up living with her dad because he happened to become quite financially stable. The second oldest is me, the middle child is Sanyiaa who exemplifies that the middle child stereotype is true but I love her anyway, the second youngest is Jyla who is usually in her own world, and finally, we have the youngest Sarii who most people say acts like me. As you can see I'm the only boy out of all five of my mom's children, most people are surprised that I'm still sane. Being the only boy and the oldest child in the household means that a lot of responsibility falls on me like babysitting, cooking,

making sure that my sisters have cleaned up and other brotherly duties. Being a single mom is hard especially with a son. My mom would often say "I can't teach you how to be a man."

This feeling has led to my mom dating some of the worst men, and she's gone from one bad relationship to another. The worst of them was this one guy, I'm not sure how they met but I do know that he had just served five years in prison. He seemed like a nice guy and he treated us good..... well at first. After about 8 months he would beat my mom and when he got drunk the beatings would get worse. The most memorable beating was when I was about 9 and my basketball coach was dropping me off home after we'd had a great practice. We were laughing and joking in the car, and as we pulled up into the driveway we could hear my mom yelling and as I got out of the car I sprinted to see what was going on. What I saw through that window is something that I will never forget. I saw him with one hand full of my mom's hair and in the other hand was a gun pointed at my mom's head while she was holding Sarii, who at the time was 18 months old. I guess he saw my coach and ran out of the house throwing the gun over the fence. At this moment I looked back at my basketball coach with tears running down my checks frozen and he asked me, "Do they usually fight like this?" I replied softly, "yes, but it's usually not this bad." I could see the shock in my coach's face or maybe it was the revelation as to why I would break down when he constantly yelled at me and why I got mad so easily.

Fast forward to about a week later, a lady from DCF came to talk to me, and this may have been my 100th time being talked to by a DCF worker, but normally my mom would tell us what to say and what not to say. However, this time she didn't. When I got home there was a grey sedan in the yard I had never seen before. I walked in the house and there was a man in the dining room, I spoke to him and my mom. I told my mom that my sisters would be inside in a little bit, because they were racing home. She didn't say anything so I went to my room and found all my things where packed. My mom shortly followed me into my room. She said "DCF is taking y'all," as my eyes began to water she said, "You're the only boy, you can't cry you have to be strong for your sisters."

There were so many questions that I wanted to ask but the words just wouldn't come out. My sisters walked into the room looking for my mom so I wiped my tears away and my mom told them what was happening. Then at the same time, we all came in for one last big hug that would have to comfort us for the next year and a half.

The lessons learned, clearly I learned to never hit women no matter how mad I get. Though this story is filled with hate and violence ironically it has taught me a lot about love. I've learned that you can't rush love, love is blind, not everyone knows how to love, and most of all that love is complicated. This has built my drive, determination, and character. It made me want to work hard in everything that I do and to always give it my best. The most important lesson that this has all taught me is to never take my family for granted. Though

I have had some challenges throughout my life, I wouldn't change a thing because it made me the driven, family oriented and understanding person that I am today.

Zachariah
Andre

18 Years Old

Tween Life...
Do over please!

- Jalia Simmons

Lesson Learned

"Do not overwhelm yourself with things that you cannot change but be more focused on making yourself a better person and being happy with who you are. Try to surround yourself with only positive people so that when you are feeling down they will help lift you up."

Life as a 16 year old Isn't the easiest thing to deal with. Most people would say "Oh your 15, so you're young and you don't really know what life is really like." But actually, life really started hitting me at the age of 13. I was living a good life and then bam something changed! To this moment I can't really explain exactly what it was, but I can tell you that I started experiencing emotions that I had never felt before.

I was going through so much stuff as a child that as I turned into a teen, I didn't really know how to react or respond to different situations. So I would just push it away or try and ignore it. I thought that by ignoring it, that meant that it didn't exist or that it didn't bother me. Not knowing that what I was doing was really making my problems bigger by acting like they didn't bother me. That wasn't really the best decision if you ask me.

I slowly started to notice myself changing, but not for the better, FOR THE WORSE. I would always be mad or sad and it would be for no reason. I eventually started to recognize that when I would start to think about what was happening in my private life I would start to feel some type of way. And not something that really doesn't make much sense to me, but stuff that I really was going through. Know what the weirdest thing is? It's that I

was never able to really identify one thing that was making me feel that way it was just a combination of a lot of different things that happened and that continued to affect me in little small ways until it really added up.

I still didn't want to talk to anyone about it because I felt that people wouldn't take me seriously or that they would judge me. Although, I did have a few people as my support team, it was that it was hard for me to share with anybody outside of a few groups of people. I knew that people who love me really care for me and would have wanted to know, but in that situation, it felt best keeping things to myself and not having to talk about it over and over again to people who would probably never understand. See from the outside everyone thought that everything was perfect. In reality, I seemed to be the girl that had everything she wanted and was doing fine and feeling good. But I was going through some hard things that I didn't understand myself.

All this was going on while I was in middle school, so I would always have a way to forget about it and just enjoy school. Acting like I was OK by hanging out with my friends, doing middle school stuff and enjoying the process of growing up in the eyes of most. But I eventually grew out of that and forgot all about it and started to let things slowly get better. I am not going to say that I helped myself but I think it's some situations that did. When things were bothering me I just begin to look at them slowly and find out ways to handle the situation. I wouldn't become so overwhelmed with little basic things anymore and I start recognizing that a lot of the issues that I was going through were all normal. I just had to find myself in the process.

Now I'm in the 9th grade and most of the things that I had to deal with, they were just temporary and I don't have to worry about them anymore. I am so glad that I recognized how to handle a lot of my issues and understood that, that was just one phase of my life. I also recognized that I had amazing supportive people around me who are willing to help me if I needed help, all I had to do is to say something and ask.

I still face some trials and tribulations but the only difference now is that I've learned how to deal with them and let them be sometimes. I am not saying that I am perfect. I do bad things, I do good things, and I am just a normal teenage girl. But one thing about it now is that I understand that there's a process for everything and it is OK for me sometimes not to be perfect, not to want things a certain way but for me just to enjoy life and accept things as they come.

Words of advice:

So if there was a word of advice that I could give anyone who may be going through this would be that if you were about to enter middle school please have a very close group of trustworthy friends or family members that you can talk to when you were going through problems. I do not know what it is about middle school but everything about me began to change and it was hard for me to accept all at once. Recognize that you're not the only one and that there are so many others who are going to find out who they are at that

age. Do not overwhelm yourself with things that you cannot change but be more focused on making yourself a better person and being happy with who you are. Try to surround yourself with only positive people so that when you are feeling down they will help lift you up. I hope that my story is able to help other young people understand that even if you are going through some of the things that I mentioned that you are not alone. This is a normal process and sometimes many of us process things differently than others. Please know that you can make it out of your situation and that one day you will be able to look back and be proud of the person that you are becoming. Lastly, it's OK not to be perfect. Just be who you are and that is good enough!

Jalia
Simmons

16 Years Old

Letting go of the Beast!

- Shakia Simmons

Lesson Learned

"Life happens to all of us, and we all need a shoulder to cry on or someone to just vent to."

There's nothing like a mother's love for their child, and a child's love for their mother. Mother's can give you your very first experience of having a best friend. In my mind most girls go to their mommy about all of their life experiences and challenges but that little girl wasn't me.

I've never been close enough to my mom to just go sit down and have a conversation with her about my life. Don't get me wrong she made it happen; I just wasn't able to sit down and tell her everything without having fears of her not being willing to accept all I had to say. I'm not sure why, considering the fact that my mom was there; but that one on one, ride or die type of relationship wasn't as strong as I need it to be. Not having that relationship with my momma caused me to be really angry and distant, and as a result I keep everything inside. I mean like, EVERYTHING. Sometimes I keep too much to myself, and this hasn't worked out to good for me.

My mom has given me the deepest love possible and she made sure that I always had more than enough. But at times, I felt like my mom was distant from me and that her focus was on other things, which made me feel left out. Instead of telling my mom this, I just began to keep things to myself. For a long time, I pushed people away, stayed to myself,

and just didn't wanna be bothered. I went through a lot at a young age which makes me hold my emotions inside, and when I explode everything comes out all at once. I mean EVERYTHING!

I got kicked out of school, lost friends, and I lost many opportunities because of my anger. Sometimes, I'm even embarrassed to share some of the things that I have done while angry. But I recognize that anger is one horrible thing to hold on to, because the longer you hold on to it, the more it grows. Angry people are not fun people to be around. I knew that being so angry was not healthy for me and one day I chose to not continue to let anger ruin my life.

I began to think about how I can help myself become better, and I recognized that talking out some of my issues could really help me. I began to do a mental survey and I recognized that I had other women in my life who were like mother figures to me, but there's no one like your momma, I mean NO ONE.

There have been times when I just needed my momma but she wasn't there to be a shoulder to cry on, a person to talk to, or a woman to ask for advice. I'm not saying that she was bad; she just had other things which took up her time. So in order to get all of this stuff out, I turned to my grandma, who is the most important woman in my life. Now my grandma is MY Beyonce, my queen, my everything, the real OG in my life: that's my granny. She is the reason why I am the young woman I am today. I talk to her about everything and she gives me solid advice, allows me to cry, scream, and just get it all out. Because of her I have learned to become a better person and let anger GO! I no longer want anger to control me. I have learned to control my anger. My grandmother has helped me become a young, black, pretty, princess, who is ambitious, confident, and intelligent. Because of her guidance and the time that she has taken with me, I know that I will be great.

If I could leave you with some advice it would be to please be sure to have someone you can talk to about the things that will happen in your life. Life happens to all of us, and we all need a shoulder to cry on or someone to just vent to. I would also like you to know that anger does not have to control YOU. YOU can control your anger!

.

Shakia Simmons

16 Years Old

13 Years and Counting

- Brashaya McCrimmon-Lampkin

Lesson Learned

"Kids in situations like mine should never worry about what others think or say about you. You didn't choose this, it chose you."

My name is Brashaya McCrimmon-Lampkin, and this is the story of my life...so far. I've been through a lot, even though I'm still young. I've learned how to take the good and the bad and make everything work for me. I've come to the realization that I can push my way through anything.

My mom was on drugs when she was pregnant with me. After 9 months of pregnancy here comes BRASHAYA! I was, if I must say so myself, a beautiful baby. During the entire pregnancy my family was concerned that my mom's drug use was going to leave me with all kinds of issues. Well, at birth I had pneumonia and I had to stay in the hospital for 4 days, my mom was sent home after 2 days. Other than that, I was a healthy baby.

My mom's boyfriend at the time that I was born was doing the same things that my mom was doing, except he also drank a lot. At the time I had 4 other siblings, 2 girls and 2 boys that were all older than me. One day my mom left all 5 of us with her boyfriend. He had no idea how to take care of us. We were with him for 3 days. That Sunday afternoon my grandma and grandpa came to visit us and when they saw us my grandma thanked my mom's boyfriend for keeping an eye on us and she took us with them. My diaper had not been changed the entire time and I had a horrible rash. My siblings had not been bathed or fed the entire time that my mom had been gone. I was 3 weeks old when this happened, I'm 13 years old now and I've been with my grandma ever since.

My mom also had another child after she had me. She was still fighting with her addiction when she had my little brother. She stayed around for 3 months after he was born, unlike the nearly 3 weeks that I got. I've sat and cried at night because my older sisters would tease me, saying that I'm not their real sister because our grandma is my mom. I've always been jealous of my mom's older kids because they actually had a really good mom, until she started using drugs.

My mom used to come and stay with us off and on. Then she would say that she was going to the doctor, or something like that, and she wouldn't come home for 5 days to a week. When my mom used to disappear I would ask a lot of questions. When she was around she used to take me around guys and tell them that I was their child to get money from them. That made me feel like I wasn't enough for her. There was even a time when my mom sold my asthma machine for money and at that point my grandma kicked her out. Seeing my mom makes me feel sad. I don't like seeing her like that, (looking like a crackhead).

When my mom was little my grandma was a drug dealer and she was on drugs too. She stopped because she wanted to change her life for her kids. She's been clean now for 23 years. Now she's my mom, my grandma and my dad. She's everything to me! She always tells me that "it's okay," whenever I would talk about my mom and start to feel sad. She tells me to pray that she gets better and not to worry when other kids talk about my mom because they don't know my mom. When kids talk about my mom I get mad, and it makes me want to fight. My mom and her boyfriend now have a duplex that they live in. She's recently gone to rehab and she looks kinda better, but I really wish that she could be a better mom.

My dad has never had been a consistent figure in my life. He has 4 other kids, 3 of them are younger than me and they're all boys. My oldest brother is in jail, 1 of my brothers is in foster care and the last 2 of my dad's kids are with him and his wife. My dad's wife doesn't like to deal with his "other" kids. I wasn't even invited to his wedding. In my entire 13 years, the most I've gotten from my dad is child support and 2 pairs of sneakers.

Kids in situations like mine should never worry about what others think or say about you. You didn't choose this, it chose you. Never give up and never put yourself in the same position. You are not your mom. You're your own person, so be your own person and you should never use drugs. There are people out here to help you to deal with the way you feel and to support you. Maybe you'll even have a grandma like I do. And if you don't there are always mentors, counselors and teachers available to help you. Just never give up, because I won't!

Brashaya
McCrimmon-Lampkin

13 Years Old

Keep Calm and Pray On!

- Zaniyah Starke

"Many people may not understand, because they are living a different life but that's OK. You keep being who you are and being the example that you were born to be."

As the last tear fell down from my face as the praise and worship music became nothing more than a distant sound, I couldn't help but ask myself, "why aren't I hanging out with my friends; cursing, drinking and listening to unholy music?"

I was always identified as the boring Christian girl, but this is not me, this is not who I am, this is not where I belong. Is this who I am? I need answers.

Bit by bit every Christian part of me started to die, until one day, when I was identified as the girl who hides and shuts the world out because of hurt pain and regret. As I started to change I developed a new body, new look, new personality, and a new me. I said, "this is me!" Peer pressure played a big part in my new life. I stopped going to church and listening to gospel music and reading the bible. "This can't be me," I said "Oh Lord, please! This trial is too hard. I'm just a child. I can't do this." I gave up and lost all hope of setting myself free from spirits that made me think I was not good enough, and then I started becoming distant from everyone I loved.

I pushed harder and harder until I started going back to church and singing the gospel, and reading the word. I started changing into Zaniyah, not the Zaniyah that other people wanted me to be, but the Zaniyah that I wanted to be. As I looked in the mirror one last time, I said, "this is me, this is where I belong, this is my answer." I'm thankful for the mercies that God has shown me. It's not easy being a Christian young lady in this day and time. So many people around you are telling you to do different things, or to be more like them.

When you do try to be who you know you are, you become the outsider. Although I have made a lot of mistakes, I have to admit that personally I feel more like myself when I'm doing the things that I know I should do. Some of my mistakes, I'm not happy about and I would never tell people about them openly. But the more I find myself, the more I recognize that I was designed to be a "God's girl."

I'm always going to try my hardest to do the things that I know I should do and to avoid the things that I know I shouldn't do; cursing and being like everyone else is not who I am, and although I have been pressured into following the paths of others; I'm glad to find my way back. If I had any words of advice for anyone who is reading this, it would be; don't be afraid of who you are and when you are "God's girl," or "God's person," that should be something that you're proud to announce to the world and not keep it to yourself. Many people may not understand, because they are living a different life but that's OK. You keep being who you are and being the example that you were born to be. Please don't do like I did trying to fit in, all it did was keep me so far away from my truth.

Luke 1:78 & 79 - Through the heartfelt mercies of our God, God's sunrise will break in upon us, shining on those in the darkness, those sitting in the shadow of death, Then showing us the way, one foot at a time, down a path of peace.

Be Blessed

Zaniyah Starke

13 Years Old

Does love hurt like this?

- Amilina Villafane

Lesson Learned

"Speak to someone and if you're scared to talk just write a letter to the person or send a text or email. Don't ever hold it in."

It was hard to go through so much pain at a young age, 16 was my age when everything started. It damaged me in the long run but I've held it in for so long that I thought it's time to let go and let the world know my story.

When I was 16, I fell in love with someone I thought I would never have an interest in. It started out amazing the laughing, the dates, and the cuddles. Two years ago I started feeling like the world was going against us our parents didn't want us together. They tried to split us up with anything they could possibly use, but we weren't giving in. Eventually, they stopped trying, knowing that we weren't going anywhere without each other. Until one day I thought maybe I'm more in love with him than he was with me, but I didn't think much of it because why would he not love me since he has been making me happy.

Everything went downhill when I caught him texting girls, I screamed, pushed him, and cried like any other female. He said he was sorry, he would stop, delete her and not talk to her again, and told me he loves me. I forgave him and dropped it then went on with my day. After that day, I didn't think it would happen again until it did. His phone kept ringing so I picked up to a woman's voice saying "Good morning baby how did you sleep?" and I went completely crazy and hung up. I

couldn't take it anymore, so I packed my stuff up and tried to leave. But it was too late he had already woken up and blocked the door. I told him to move, he kept asking me why am I leaving and what did he do. I simply gave him his phone back and he saw who called, I don't know what happened to him but I know he wasn't in his right mind. He started screaming at me for touching his phone, I told him I wouldn't have touched it if his girlfriend didn't call.

He kept going and going and I wasn't having it still so I tried to leave again when he had a walk to the room...that was the last time I've seen the boy I fell in love with. He grabbed my bag and threw it to the other side of the room, I instantly got scared and ran out the door but I didn't make it far. He ran out and grabbed me and took me back inside, right at that very moment I was terrified.

He held me until he locked the door and closed all the windows and blinds, he threw me on the floor slap me and punch me around. I couldn't leave the house until I was all healed up. But I couldn't leave alone I had to be with him everywhere he was just for him to make sure I didn't tell anyone.

Three years in and I'm not affected by it anymore. I walk around these streets alone not speaking about it cause at the end of the day I'm the only one getting hurt. Fake smiles and laughs all day long, It's what I had to do to make sure I don't get hit. There was no telling how worse he could hurt me. And I didn't want to find out. I always ask myself Why am I not dead? How is my body taking all this beating? How is my body functioning with so much blood lost?. I didn't know how to answer these questions and I couldn't talk to no one about it knowing that at the end of the day, I was going to suffer the consequences. It's going to be the end of 3 years now and I am no longer afraid of the abuse. people might say that's bad you're going to get yourself hurt keeping this in, but in reality, I'm getting hurt regardless if I speak about it or not. I get hit for little things now. Him knowing he has control over me is a drug to him and he's addicted to it.

We play a happy couple in front of his family, my family, friends, and anyplace else, tell cute relationship stories as if they were really true and take cute pictures as if we were really going to hang them up. But once we're indoors, I'm most likely getting hit or screamed at for saying or doing something wrong. It could've been so little as of me talking to someone without him being next to me.

I honestly felt that this was my life now. And I hated it. I came to an understanding that I was only getting out of this situation one way, and that was by killing myself.

There was one day he hit me for calling him a cheater because he was texting five other girls. After he hit me, he locked me in the room and left. I was already bleeding so I decided to do something I never did before; I didn't want to live anymore. I had a glass bottle in the room, so I broke it and got the biggest and sharpest piece I saw. I didn't think about everything and everyone I was leaving behind, I just wanted the pain to stop so I cut my wrist, I felt all the pain go away. Until

he came back and saw me. He took it away and held me. I didn't know how to feel, but I know it was fake love and I wasn't going to get pulled back in.

I came to the fact that I needed to speak to someone, I have a group of friends at school that I talk to them about everything, so I finally spoke up and told them and after I cried and got held and supported. After that, they kept me away from him.

I am now 19 turning 20 and I have moved on from him completely. I have amazing friends, 2 jobs, graduated high school, and getting my career started early.

I never knew what happy felt like, until I finally spoke up and those close to me helped me get away. He can no longer control or touch me. I have grown to be my own independent woman with goals and empowerment. No one can or will stop me.

If you ever feel or are in this type of situation, my advice is to speak up even if you're scared. Once you tell someone and ask for help, they'll find a way to get you away from that person.

Don't ever hold it in. That was my mistake and it resolved to me getting abused for 3 years and I easily could've been free if I spoke up earlier. I know you're scared, but taking your life isn't an option. I know exactly how you feel. You feel as if you're stuck forever and the only way out is suicide, but it's not. Speak to someone and if you're scared to talk just write a letter to the person or send a text or email. Don't ever hold it in.

You're going to love it when you speak up. You're going to finally feel free, happy, and feel like no one can stop you.

Hi, my name is Amilina. I am now free and happy.

Amilina
Villafane

19 Years Old

The setback prepared me for a comeback!

- Jefferson Bassy

Lesson Learned

"Don't let the negativity bring you in, make it your strength and overcome it."

Growing up in Parramore, people thought I wouldn't be successful because of the violence in my community. From the start, I knew I wanted to get out of it and be successful. Being the youngest is an awesome experience because you have a person that is guiding you along the way. I grew up with 2 brothers who both of them graduated high school and now in college. I had no choice to do the same but in a greater way. My parents didn't play about education and I had a certain time I had to be in the house. I had two (2) choices which were focusing on getting good grades or being drawn into the negativity that people say about Parramore.

Most people either end up dead or in jail. Hanging out with certain friends I knew there was a limit for them. Being successful was the only thing on my mind. I played football at Jones High School for all 4 years. My junior year of high school I made the varsity team. I didn't have the chance to start because there was a senior in front of me. It was October 23, 2017, where I got injured at practice. I thought I wouldn't be able to walk or play football during my senior year of high school. On November 9, 2017, I received surgery because I have torn my ACL and Meniscus. I was depressed for a while and my grades dropped instantly. I was on crutches for at least 3 months. My mentor Brad Mason told me to keep moving don't let it sit and that's what I did. It was 2 weeks after my surgery I started working out again. I would go with "The Give Team" which is the only inner obstacle city team in Orlando. He created a separate workout for me so I was able to do it.

Fast forward into 2018, I was going through therapy and still doing things that they said I couldn't do because I knew I could do it but being cautious with it. With the help of the Lord, I was able to get through it and was able to walk again and play football during my Senior year of high school. I was surrounded with people who helped and cared about me which they pushed me through the process. "If you want to go fast, go alone. If you want to go far, go together." This is my favorite quote because this is true about life. Another quote I also love is "Life is a team sport. DRAFT ACCORDINGLY!" You choose who you want to be in your life. This is why it's true. My message to leave with you guys is; always remember to stay close with the Lord and explore the world. Don't let the negativity bring you in, make it your strength and overcome it. I will be attending Morehouse College because of the hard work I've put in and I never gave up on myself even though I wanted to.

Jefferson
Bassy

19 Years Old

"

Young but Resilient!

— Libby Sims

" Yes, things may have been hard, and yes there are things that I'm yet waiting to happen in my life but I'm also very aware that I'm not going to let those things hinder me and stop me from being the person that I need to be."

My name is Libby Sims and I'm 14 years old. I come from a loving and caring family, but not everything with them has always been perfect. I have four younger brothers and I'm the oldest child for both my mother and my father. I live with my mom and one of my brothers. It hasn't always been easy for me, but I have learned to make the best out of life. At one point in my life things were HARD.

I remember going from hotel to hotel, moving from house to house; staying with family members or with some of my mom's friends. My mom was always willing to do what she had to do for us, but I know that at some point things just became overwhelming for her as she was a single mother trying to raise my brother and me.

I remember being the in the sixth grade and catching the city bus with my little brother to and from school while my mom would be at work. Of course you know that by me being the oldest sibling that meant that I had to look after him and make sure that he was OK. After school we would also catch the bus to our after school program at New Image Youth Center praying that we would be able to make it back home safely. At times I would sit down and cry, wondering why my life was so different from my friends. To me their lives were totally different from mine and it

appeared that they had everything that they needed and wanted. That wasn't the case with me and my brother. We had what we needed, but our wants was a totally different story. It was to the point where I felt that I couldn't be happy. So I wasn't. I made myself mad thinking about all the stuff that I didn't have. I would wake up with an attitude and go to sleep with an attitude and I wouldn't want to do anything. I remember seeing my mom working countless jobs to take care of us. I was grateful but I was still MAD.

We didn't always have nice clothes or shoes like I thought we should have. I would call my dad and try to ask him to get me and my brother things to help my mom out but he would never pull through. He would always disappoint us and make up an excuse or just not come through at all. I feel like because of my dad not being there in the way that I thought he should, that I was missing something in life. To this day there's a big hole missing in my heart which really bothers me sometimes. But hey, I can't force my dad to want a relationship with us right? I'm definitely not over it and my heart still aches for the relationship that I hope that one day we can have. Because of this pain sometimes I can't sleep at night. There are times when I have been in the shower and I would just cry and as the water would fall from the showerhead the tears would also fall from my eyes. Sometimes I wasn't even sure what was producing the most water the shower or me releasing all of my pain through my tears. Sometimes I would try to make myself feel better by thinking that, my father not being in my life could be a good thing. Maybe right now he's not ready to be the father that I need for him to be and maybe if he did come around I would only be disappointed. I would rather wait for the perfect time so that when the relationship is ready it will be strong and I will be able to have everything that I have always wanted from my father. At least that's my prayer.

My family always tells me not to rush it, and that he will come around sooner or later. I see other kids go through some of the same things that I'm going through in my life. I've often wondered if they know that they are not the only ones experiencing the things that they're going through. That's one of the main reasons why I wanted to write a chapter in this book, because I want other children, especially teenagers, to know that you may have problems but I promise you you're not the only one. Although it appears that everybody else may have it better than you, because they smile more than you and appear to be happy all of the time. But, you never know what's going on behind closed doors. Remember that a lot of people know how to wear smiles in order to cover up what's really taking place on the inside.

If I could give you some advice, I would want you to know that you're not the only one going through. We all have our own inner battles that we're fighting. Yes, things may have been hard, and yes there are things that I'm yet waiting to happen in my life but I'm also very aware that I'm not going to let those things hinder me and stop me from being the person that I need to be. I'm a fun, energetic, beautiful, young girl who loves to laugh, make friends and help other people. All of these things make me unique and they make me who I am. One of my goals is to make a difference in my community some day and help out the kids that have the same issues that I have. My advice to other girls and boys is to keep striving towards your goals and don't let NOTHING bring you down. Pray and put God first in all of your situations and don't let yourself down and don't let anyone else either. I may not be perfect, and I may not have a perfect life, but I am going to live my best life starting now.

Libby
Sims

14 Years Old

To all Youth

We hope that the stories and various pieces in this book have become some-thing more to you than just words put on the paper.

It is each and every one of our youth authors desire to encourage you to never give up no matter what lesson life is teaching you.

It is their goal to give you hope, and to remind you that you are not alone should you encounter some of these same issues during your young years.

Thank you so much for reading and supporting those who are ready to let it all out.